Leverage Your Laziness!

Leverage Your Laziness!

How to do what you love, ALL THE TIME!

sound wisdom
Shippensburg, PA

Sound Wisdom
167 Walnut Bottom Road
Shippensburg, PA 17257

www.soundwisdom.com

This book and all other Sound Wisdom books are available at bookstores and distributors worldwide.

ISBN 13: 978-1-937879-14-3
ISBN Ebook: 978-1-937879-15-0

For Worldwide Distribution, Printed in the U.S.A.

2 3 4 5 6 7 / 16 15 14 13

Acknowledgements

From Steve: This book is not merely my advice to others; it is my mantra and my credo. Therefore, almost by definition, my thanks go out to all the other people who made my "lazy life" possible. This list includes virtually everyone I know. While I am leveraging my own laziness, which in my case means doing nothing but talking, these people keep all of the other fires burning that make my life possible.

I must begin by acknowledging Jeff Goldberg and Brandon Toropov, without whom you would not be reading this book; instead, you would have heard me talk about how someday, I planned to get around to it.

Also, thanks to Michael Durand and Neil Rothstein who really invented the concept of leveraging laziness as a way to reach success—without them, there would have been nothing to write about.

Thanks also to my business partners, David Moore, Michael Flannery and Tom Mahar, with whom I have been able to build an actual business around my strengths. This has to be the essence of laziness leveraged.

Special thanks go to my wife Fran Proto, a serial entrepreneur who wouldn't know laziness if it hit her. Without her, I would have written *How to be Lazy (and broke!)* on a paper bag—or maybe I would have just put it off.

And heartfelt thanks go to my daughter Brittany Bookbinder, whose own philosophy appears to be *Leverage Your Talent with Hard Work;* her shining example of pursuing her life's goal is a constant motivation to me.

Thanks in advance to all of you who recommend this book to others. I would tell them myself, but I'm too... well, you get the picture.

From Jeff: Lazy is where it's at! Take it from someone who knows... me. If you think Steve is lazy you should hang out with me for a day... then you'll see what real lazy is all about!

Of course, being this lazy means getting good help. This is where I tell you that this book, like our previous book "How to Be Your Own Coach," (www.byourowncoach.com) would never have been written if not for my dear friend Steve Bookbinder and our editing pal, Brandon Toropov. My gratitude goes out to both of them.

Thanks go, too, to all the grammar school teachers who told me I'd never amount to anything because I was "full of potential but just too lazy to ever succeed." Their lack of encouragement and foresight weren't exactly an inspiration, but they did serve as an important motivating factor.

I am also grateful to some of my smarter employers over the years—the ones who encouraged my particular brand of laziness and realized that sometimes you've just got to trust your gut and let people be who they are—even though doing so means your employees might not fit into the conventional mold.

Many thanks, too, go to my oldest, and dearest, friend Ken Wilensky and to his law partner Michael Vessa. Ken and Michael are great role models, two people who have been leveraging their laziness quite successfully for the last 30 years or so.

I also want to thank my dog Dora. No one understands how to leverage laziness better than a pug.

My deepest thanks go to my children, Zachary, Skylar, and Avery. They teach me constantly what life is really all about. (If you're wondering, life is about love, hugs and kisses.) They never fail to amaze me; every day, they prove just how much you can learn from someone under the age of ten.

Finally, like Steve, I want to send out a huge thank you to you, the reader. Without you, we'd just be a couple of lazy guys expounding our ideas to each other on my couch instead of being wealthy (in so many ways) beyond our wildest dreams. Thanks for buying this book.

Contents

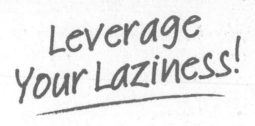

Introduction

"So you see, imagination needs moodling—long, inefficient, happy idling, dawdling and puttering."

~ BRENDA UELAND

Why a book about laziness?

Because most people actually get their best work done when they're being lazy. It's the lack of laziness in their lives that keeps them from achieving what they could, and should, be achieving. Sometimes it takes a lifetime to learn that about yourself. This book is here to help you accelerate the process.

What most people call "lazy," we call "life as it was meant to be lived."

This book is for you if...

- You know all about the rule, "Never put off until tomorrow what you could do today..." but you end up putting off important stuff anyway.

- You've ever thought to yourself, or said out loud, something like the following: "As soon as I (insert activity you don't really like very much here), then I'll move on to the task of making headway on my major goals in life."

- You're a "big picture" person who is lousy at the details.

- You're a "details" person who is lousy at the "big picture."

- The sheer enormity of some of your goals sometimes keeps you from taking any action at all, because you just don't know how to, or have any idea where to, start.

- You have lots of great ideas, but somehow never move forward on—or finish most of them.
- You feel you are halfway toward achieving balance in your life—the half that includes doing exactly what you want to do, when you want to do it—but you still feel there's something missing.

We believe that, at some level, all of us are lazy. Some of us are capable of acknowledging our own unique brand of laziness, and leveraging it. Others do a pretty good job of concealing laziness—by pretending that they like to do stuff that they actually wish they could put off doing forever.

We believe that pretending you're not lazy is a recipe for an unhappy life.

What if there was a way to put off all the stuff you didn't want to do... starting immediately... and then continue to put that stuff off for the rest of your life? Without, y'know, going to jail or anything?

Well, there is. We call it leveraging your laziness—embracing your inner lazy bum.

The most successful people in the world have figured out how to leverage their laziness. And, amazingly enough, a couple of lazy bums like us have figured it out, too. We figure that if we could understand this, pretty much anyone could. So we wrote this book to share the neglected art of leveraging your own laziness with the whole world.

Anyone can learn to build their lives around doing what they want to do, and avoiding all the other stuff. But there is a catch. You have to know what you like doing most, and be willing to ask yourself, over and over again, how you can find ways to do it more and more often.

This requires getting to know yourself.

And now, a confession. To open this book, we originally planned to ask you 25 different, complex self-discovery questions as an opening assessment piece—something that would help you get a clearer fix on what you actually like doing. Then we realized that you, our audience, are lazy people like us. And we realized that we, ourselves, hate taking tests, and would do just about anything to avoid them. (Well, Steve hates taking tests, but Jeff enjoys them.)

Anyway, we kept it simple. We boiled the whole self-assessment piece into three simple sentences. Just complete the three phrases below, in as much or as little detail as you feel is appropriate. If you want to write down the complete phrases, you can do that. If you're too lazy to write, just say the answers out loud to someone you love and trust. And if even that is a bit of a stretch, given your personal laziness profile, tear this page out of the book and tape it to your head for a couple of minutes as you do something else. Then, whenever you feel like it, pull the sheet off your forehead, take another look at it... and see what comes your way.

1. Even if nobody paid me to do it, I would still....

_____

_____

2. Time flies when I am helping someone to....

_____

_____

3. If I were the central character of a major
    Hollywood film, my character would....

_____

_____

Once you have pondered the
endings of these three incomplete
questions for exactly as long as you
feel like pondering them... and not
one second longer... turn the page.

Leverage Your Laziness!

Principle #1:
Don't Listen to What The Man Said!

"The devil finds work for idle hands."

~ THE MAN

Most people listen to what The Man said. And that's a shame.

If you spend enough time listening to The Man— you know, the pervasive, immortal authority figure who wants you to live your life pretty much the way everyone else does—then a terrible thing will eventually happen to you. You'll come to believe that laziness, as we're defining it—that is, avoiding things you suck at doing or don't want to do—is antisocial, immoral, or (even worse) fattening behavior.

We have another word for true laziness: genius!

In support of our definition, we submit, for your consideration, some real-life quotes from real-life experts on the subject. Below, you will find some critical insights on work and laziness from some truly remarkable people—people who chose to write their own ticket in life and chose not to listen to what The Man said. Before you start repeating what The Man said—which most people are all too happy to repeat about laziness ask yourself: What did these people know that The Man somehow overlooked?

"It's true hard work never killed anybody, but I figure, why take the chance?"

~Ronald Reagan

*"It does not seem to be true that work necessarily
needs to be unpleasant. It may always have to
be hard, or at least harder than doing nothing
at all. But there is ample evidence that work
can be enjoyable and that, indeed, it is often the
most enjoyable part of life."*

~ **MIHALY CSIKSZENTMIHALYI,** *Author of*
Flow: The Psychology of Optimal Experience

*"Whenever there is a hard job to be done I
assign it to a lazy man; he is sure to find an easy
way of doing it."*

~ **WALTER CHRYSLER**

"Eighty percent of success is showing up."

~ **WOODY ALLEN**

*"I don't think necessity is the mother of
invention - invention, in my opinion, arises
directly from idleness, possibly also from laziness.
To save oneself trouble."*

~ **AGATHA CHRISTIE**

"Far from idleness being the root of all evil, it is rather the only true good."

~ SOREN KIERKEGAARD

"Efficiency is intelligent laziness."

~ DAVID DUNHAM

"All paid jobs absorb and degrade the mind."

~ ARISTOTLE (384 BC - 322 BC)

"One of the symptoms of an approaching nervous breakdown is the belief that one's work is terribly important."

~ BERTRAND RUSSELL

"Working gets in the way of living."

~ OMAR SHARIF

"If hard work were such a wonderful thing, surely the rich would have kept it all to themselves."

~ LANE KIRKLAND

Do these people sound like they spent a lot of time listening to The Man?

The Man has his reasons for wanting us to spend our time and effort, and indeed our lives doing things we suck at doing.

Yet clearly... these people weren't listening to The Man—and they seem to have done all right for themselves.

If they didn't have to listen to what The Man said... *we* don't have to listen to what The Man said!

In this book, we are challenging you to undertake a great mission; a mission that all of the fascinating, successful people whose ideas you just read understood and accepted. It is identifying, and profiting from, your own special variety of laziness. It is the mission that erases the boundary between work and play. It is the mission that rewards the truly lazy person. This mission, we believe, is as sacred as anything in human experience, and the only true marker for success in life. Completing this mission is easy, not hard, and it gives you the right to say, in no uncertain terms, "I choose not to do that which I do not enjoy, and I will take my chances with what I do enjoy."

YOU find out what makes the most sense to do with idle hands. Not the devil. In fact, that's one of the first steps to finding your own special variety of laziness: By letting your hands go idle for a while.

Don't wimp out. Keep reading. We call the whole process of finding your own special variety of laziness reverse-engineering. You'll learn about this in the next chapter.

Leverage Your Laziness!

Principle #2:
Reverse Engineering
is a Lifetime Project

*"A man is a success if he gets up in the morning
and gets to bed at night, and in between
he does what he wants to do."*

~ BOB DYLAN

Like a lot of great ideas, the "leverage your laziness" idea has its appealing and unappealing aspects.

The appealing part, which we hope is quite obvious to you already, is that you get to live your life on

your own terms, which is, for most of us, an energizing prospect. In fact, we'd be willing to bet that
when you understood what we really mean by the
word "lazy," it felt intuitively right to you. Maybe
you read what some of the great "lazy" minds had
to say about the subject in the previous chapter, or
what Bob Dylan had to say at the beginning of this
one, and you thought to yourself, "Hey—they're
right! That IS what real success is."

Then there comes the less appealing side. If you're
like most of the people we've worked with, about two
seconds after you realized how exciting this idea was,
you then thought to yourself, "Yeah—it sounds good.
But the problem is, I don't have the slightest clue how
to pull this off."

Fortunately, that's about to change.

Here's how you pull it off: By reverse-engineering your life—which means noticing what
works and makes you feel good. Reverse-engineering your life simply means getting into the habit of
noticing what you really want to do and enjoy doing... and then finding some way to do that, big or

small, every single day that you are above ground, as much as you possibly can.

Couldn't be simpler, right? Right! If you do that, you'll be all set. Who needs the rest of this book? You've now got everything you could possibly need. Go forth and laze.

Just in case you do want to keep reading, though... you should follow us carefully through this next part, because it's where most people slip up.

You really can travel from the place you are now to the place that you know, deep down inside, that you want to go—the place where you can actually leverage your laziness—*if* you can accept one simple guiding principle in your life. How far you get on this path depends on how terrified you feel when you encounter this principle. Here it is:

You, and you alone, can reverse-engineer yourself.

Get used to this principle. Repeat it to yourself regularly, until it stops feeling terrifying. Say it out loud right now. No, really, SAY IT! Or we'll find you and make you say it.

"I, and I alone, can reverse-engineer myself."

Did you say it? If you didn't, you're a wimp, and we're on our way over right now to kick your ass. If you did say it, right out loud so people, including you, could hear—congratulations. You're on the path. *Keep* repeating this on a daily basis.

There is no other expert on this topic. There is no one else on earth who can make finding out what you want to do, finding out what you enjoy doing, finding out what you are good at doing, your priority. There is no one else who can put what you want to do onto your schedule, whether for five minutes or five hours. There is no one else who can evaluate what's working in your life and what isn't. The process we call reverse-engineering really is up to you, and you alone.

And that's not all. Even though you're the only one who can pull this off, you're never going to get it exactly right. You are, and you will always be, a work in progress. Your own work in progress. You're never going to be "done" with this job.

Does that suck, or what?

Well, maybe not so much. The cool thing is that, once you accept that you, and you alone, can reverse engineer yourself the job actually becomes much easier. You stop trying to fob the job off on someone else. And once you accept that it's the work of a lifetime, you stop trying to get it done by Tuesday at 2:00.

Your job has two components: to *keep noticing things* and *keep moving forward* with the job of reverse-engineering your own life. We'll show you how to do that as you make your way through the book. For now, just remember this:

> Don't wimp out.
> Read this next part twice.

- **Reverse-engineering your life simply means getting into the habit of noticing what you really want to do and enjoy doing...**

- ... and then finding some way to do that, as much as possible, every single day that you are above ground.
- You do not have to have the job of reverse engineering complete by Tuesday at 2:00.
- But... you do have to decide whether you are willing to move forward on this reverse engineering thing, a little bit every day.

Leverage Your Laziness!

Principle #3:
How You Feel About What You Do Matters

"Write only what you love, and love what you write. The key word is love. You have to get up in the morning and write something you love, something to live for."

~ RAY BRADBURY

Bradbury was writing for writers, but his advice is relevant to every human being drawing breath on this earth. You cannot effectively leverage your laziness unless you love what you are doing—what you are living for. When you are doing something you love, something you truly live for, you don't *feel* like you're working... because you're not working. When you're doing something you were born to do, you're in love with that "something." It's something you could spend all day doing without ever feeling as though you were being forced to do it. But there's a catch... *Only you can determine what this "something" is.*

Forget about what your boss feels you do best. Or your parents. Or your spouse. Or your clients. Or your sixth-grade high-school English teacher. *You* are the one whose opinion matters now. The question is— what do you really love doing most? *What do you feel best doing?* Give your best answer right now.

I feel best when I'm... *(fill in the blank.)*

_____

_____

Careful! If you're tempted to fill in that blank with something someone else thinks is good for you to do, or is boring, or is something you can only do with the lights off in private, put that nominee aside for the moment. You can come back to these diversions later. What we're talking about now is what you personally feel good doing. What is it you would want to do most in life if you could do anything? What makes you feel best? What would you do if money didn't matter?

How *you* feel about your life's mission is the only thing that matters.

For right now, forget about whether what you feel best doing is "practical." (There's a dirty word if there ever was one!) Before you move on to the next chapter, identify at least one activity, passion, or pursuit that you:

a) really, truly feel great doing *and*

b) can describe, with a straight face, as your mission in life.

This may take a few minutes. Invest the time. If you're tempted to move on to the next chapter before you've *quite* figured this one out, read the quotes below until you get your mojo working.

"Happiness is the meaning and the purpose of life, the whole aim and end of human existence."

~ ARISTOTLE

"*Be happy. It's one way of being wise.*"

~ SIDONIE GABRIELLE

"*You just have to do your own thing, no matter what anyone says. It's your life.*"

~ ETHAN EMBRY

Don't wimp out. Come up with something you love doing, and believe you were put on earth to do, before you move on to the next chapter.

Leverage Your Laziness!

Principle #4:
Your Corner Of the
Universe Is Sacred

*"You aren't wealthy until you have
something money can't buy."*

~ GARTH BROOKS

I f you've made it this far in the book, you are ready
for the next challenge. We want you to get very
clear on something that you love to do—*and* that you
could someday see yourself doing. Jerry Garcia was

once asked whether he wanted to be remembered as the best guitar player who ever lived. He answered that he wanted to be remembered as the *only* guitar player who did exactly what he did. You don't have to do the thing you do "better" than anyone else. You simply have to do YOUR best, which is going to be something uniquely yours.

The idea is to find something you're really good at doing, love doing, and can see yourself doing to the very best of your ability, for fulfillment and, perhaps, profit. That's called mastery, and it starts with summoning your own personal (and most enjoyable) best on a regular basis. Who knows where that might take you?

Once you make attaining *your own personal best* something you enjoy, you've got a fix on something money can't buy. You've got your own, personal corner of the universe: the place where miracles (and laziness) happen, the place where you, and you alone, do what you do best. And that place, my friend, is sacred. Why is knowing this sacred? Because it's your key to a meaningful (i.e., lazy) life spent doing *exactly* what you want, not what someone else wants.

Let us share an example with you that may help you to get a clearer idea of what we're talking about. The great American novelist Norman Mailer grew up in a Jewish neighborhood in Brooklyn in the 1930s. Once, a reporter asked Mailer why he'd never written a book about what it was like to grow up in Brooklyn during that time period. Mailer's answer was simple, straightforward, and a model of *leveraged laziness.* He said, in so many words, "I only take on writing projects when I know for sure that no one else could imitate. There are already too many books out about growing up in Brooklyn."

Take a moment now to get clear on what you love to do, and what you could see yourself doing *repeatedly,* in your own way. If you have to invest a half an hour or so of lazy contemplation on this point—say, while you're driving from one place to another—invest that time in yourself before you move on to the next chapter.

What is your corner of the universe? Does it feel sacred to you when you think about it? Does it feel like your mission in life?

_____

_____

_____

_____

_____

"We are what we repeatedly do. Excellence, then, is not an act, but a habit."

~ ARISTOTLE

"Just make up your mind at the very outset that your work is going to stand for quality... that you are going to stamp a superior quality upon everything that goes out of your hands, that whatever you do shall bear the hallmark of excellence."

~ ORISON SWETT MARDEN

*"Striving for excellence motivates you; striving
for perfection is demoralizing."*

~ **HARRIET BERYL BRAIKER**

Don't wimp out. Expand on, or
change, what you figured out in the
last chapter. Think of something
you not only love doing, but could
see yourself mastering.

You will not be forced to eat live
crickets if you change your mind
again later on.

Leverage Your Laziness!

Principle #5:
There Is No "Off" Switch

"True genius sees with the eyes of a child and thinks with the brain of a genie."

~ **PUZANT KEVORK THOMAJAN**

*D*oing only what you do best, and only on your own terms, can be described either as being lazy... or as being a genius. If you want, you can think of it as genius. (We choose genius.) Whichever label you decide to use, your goal should be to *do more and more of the stuff you do best, ...each and every day.*

We call this process *removing the off switch on the genius machine.*

In the classic *The Lord of the Rings,* the wizard, Gandalf, is criticized for being late for an appointment. His response is priceless. Unfortunately, in order for us to quote it for you verbatim, we'd have to get permission from the estate of J.R.R. Tolkien, the author of *The Lord of the Rings*—and frankly, that's too much trouble. (We're too lazy!) So you know what we're going to do instead? We're going to paraphrase Gandalf's reply, because, as it happens, one of us is really good at paraphrasing things. (Don't ask which one.)

Gandalf's reply, paraphrased, for laziness's sake: **Wizards can't be late. In order for them to be wizards, in the real sense of that word, they must adopt the attitude that they always arrive on time—because they *only* arrive exactly when they mean to. The minute they start apologizing for being late, they stop being wizards.**

In other words, Gandalf (the character—and for that matter J.R.R. Tolkien, his creator)—didn't make mistakes. In fact, it gets even better: *By definition, Gandalf was incapable of making mistakes.* His Genius Machine was always ON. When something went "wrong," he saw only the opportunity for new wizardry. That's what geniuses do. They expand the zones in their life where labels like "wrong," "late," "should," "bad," and so on, simply don't apply. So it's impossible to imagine Gandalf feeling guilty about being late, or beating himself up for being late, or wasting any time blaming anyone else for being late. It's impossible to imagine him screwing up. *He never screws up. He's a Wizard.* (No, we're not cheerleaders for habitual lateness —see the next chapter on Accountability.)

Follow us here. Geniuses are like Gandalf. They're lazy, and they *live* in the Genius Zone. That means (for instance) that they're never late—they always show up when they mean to show up. They don't make mistakes—they take interesting detours. They see EVERYTHING as an opportunity. They don't waste time regretting or looking back—they keep moving forward. They do this *all the time.* The minute they stop spending time in the Genius Zone— the minute they stop being lazy—they stop being Geniuses!

You're only on Principle #5, so it's probably a little much for us to ask you to make the Genius Zone occupy all of your waking hours. Our question for you is: How much of the day do you spend *right now,* doing what you know you love to do and are good at doing, with your Genius Machine locked into the ON position? And how much of the day do you spend apologizing, regretting, unhappying, or belating? We made those last two verbs up, by the way. We get to. We're lazy. (And we're geniuses. Humble ones, at that.)

Start by spending at least THIRTY MINUTES, TODAY, with your Genius Machine locked in the ON position. Do not continue on to the next chapter until you've spent at least that much time without apology, preconception, or regret. Spend that thirty minutes doing *only* what you love doing, and as though it were impossible for you to make a mistake while doing it.

If you love painting, spend a lazy half-hour just painting—and doing absolutely nothing "wrong." DO IT TODAY. (Now would be best.)

If you love writing, spend a lazy half-hour writing—and doing absolutely nothing "wrong." DO IT TODAY. (Now would be best.)

If you love designing great living spaces for yourself or other people, spend a half-hour today doing ONLY that. Brainstorm. Get creative. DO IT TODAY. (Now would be best.) And do it for at least half an hour.

If you catch yourself thinking, even once, "OOPS—I made a mistake," START OVER... and keep going until you complete at least thirty minutes in the GENIUS ZONE.

Your goal is to EXPAND the amount of time you spend in the Genius Zone, doing what you were born to do. At the very least, you will now commit yourself to a minimum of thirty minutes in guilt-free, Gandalf-like wizardry, every day, with no mistakes, no matter what. If for some reason you find yourself tempted to do something you suck at doing during this period, PUT YOUR HANDS UP, BACK AWAY FROM THE ACTIVITY IN QUESTION, AND EASE YOURSELF BACK INTO THE GENIUS ZONE.

Keep it up, day after day, and you'll make the Genius Zone your guiding reality. It's the place where the fun is, where the energy is, where the *real you* is. **Eventually, you will discover that there really is no "OFF" switch on your personal Genius Machine.**

"A man's errors are his portals of discovery."

~ JAMES JOYCE

"Success seems to be connected with action. Successful people keep moving."

~ CONRAD HILTON

"Anyone who has never made a mistake has never tried anything new."

~ ALBERT EINSTEIN

*"What do you first do when you learn to swim?
You make mistakes, do you not? And what
happens? You make other mistakes, and when
you have made all the mistakes you possibly can
without drowning - and some of them many
times over - what do you find? That you can
swim. Well - life is just the same as learning to
swim! Do not be afraid of making mistakes, for
there is no other way of learning how to live!"*

~ ALFRED ADLER

Don't wimp out. Invest half an
hour in your personal Genius Zone
before you continue on to the next
chapter—and be sure to keep the
Genius Switch in the ON position.

Leverage Your Laziness!

Principle #6:
First Things First

"When work, commitment, and pleasure all become one and you reach that deep well where passion lives, nothing is impossible."

~ Anonymous

Leveraging your laziness will probably mean making fewer promises to others and... more promises to yourself to pursue your own creative path.

Leveraging your laziness means refusing to make any more commitments you can't, or won't keep...

and making new commitments to yourself to invest more of your precious time in moments of exploration and discovery.

Your commitments and promises should support what you do best. Eventually, you want all of your commitments to lead you to the zone where work, commitment, and pleasure all become one—the zone we call being lazy. We don't much care what you call that zone—but we do want you to become accountable to yourself for spending more and more time in this creative place as you make your way through this book.

Steve once did a stand-up comedy routine about a motivational speaker whose mission was to get people to do less in their lives. He delivered a fiery speech pointing out that most of the overachievers we spend our time trying so hard to imitate are actually dead—so what does that tell you? It was a funny, crazy routine, but there's a piece of good advice within it. We all tend to do too much! Our to-do lists and calendars are out of control. We have to make a conscious effort to create room for ourselves.

When you're trying to get too much done, when you take on one too many commitments, it's like trying to get onto a subway car that's already jammed with people. If you get in, you're still stuck in place and can't move. What if your goal was to empty out the car? What if you wanted to find more time in the day with which to do nothing? What if the thing that went onto your to-do list was, "Be lazy for 30 minutes this morning?" By "doing less," you could actually end up finding opportunities to do a lot more with your life. That's the paradox: If you can't start doing less, you get stuck in the subway car of your own to-do list—and you can't really expect anything more out of yourself!

Think of time management as being like a room in a tiny apartment with a floor that's crowded with books, furniture, newspapers, and other objects. Every item on your to-do list is an object on that floor. If you were to bring a sleeping bag into that room, you would have to push some stuff out of the way to give yourself some space to lie down. In so doing, you're giving the sleeping bag more space, and moving, reorganizing, or maybe even throwing away some of the other things on the floor. That's what we need to do with our day: move some stuff around, or even throw some stuff away, to make some room for the laziness we need in our lives.

First things first: Your most important responsibility is to create a "lazy space" for yourself. *Keep this promise to yourself first.*

Start reducing the total number of promises you make to others, and you'll find that you win yourself the time to follow through on the promises you do make. Most people make lots of promises they have no intention, or way, of keeping. We're not suggesting you shouldn't make promises... but we are suggesting you make promises that serve you, and that you intend to keep.

You have to make sure one of the people you're promising your time, commitment, energy, and attention to is **you**. Once you make a commitment to yourself to make room for something that excites you, something that energizes you, something that you know you were meant to experiment with boldly and discover more fully—you will find it easier to follow through on your commitments! Get your priorities straight. Find a place to put your sleeping bag—and then lie down in your lazy space, every day.

"The mind, ever the willing servant, will respond to boldness, for boldness, in effect, is a command to deliver mental resources."

~ NORMAN VINCENT PEALE

"There is a fountain of youth: It is your mind, your talents, the creativity you bring in your life and the lives of people you love."

~ SOPHIA LOREN

"A hunch is creativity trying to tell you something."

~ FRANK CAPRA

"Creativity can solve almost any problem. The creative act, the defeat of habit by originality overcomes everything."

~ GEORGE LOIS

"It's hard for corporations to understand that creativity is not just about succeeding. It's about experimenting and discovering."

~ GORDON MACKENZIE

Don't wimp out now—make a "first things first" commitment that gets you the "lazy space" you need over the next week. Set aside at least seven time slots over the next seven days when you can pursue what you do best for at least thirty uninterrupted minutes. Then... follow thorugh on your commitment!

Leverage Your Laziness!

Principle #7:
Get Passionate About Laziness

"Above all, be true to yourself, and if you cannot put your heart in it, take yourself out of it."

~ ANONYMOUS

Most of us spend all of our time working in our business, as opposed to working ON our business, and we're surprised that our business never improves. Of course it's important to work "in" your business... it's how you get paid. But when you take the time to work "on" your business as well, you'll reap great rewards. Taking the time to do nothing but think about, "How can I do things better? Differently? More productively? More efficiently?" takes practice but brings substantial gains. When Jeff committed to spending three hours per week, doing nothing but thinking about how to improve his business, creative ideas started flowing... and his business took off!

"Efficiency is intelligent laziness."

~ DAVID DUNHAM

Getting **passionate about laziness** simply means leveraging what you know about *what should happen next in a process that you've already done a lot of thinking about.*

For instance: Someone in our circle knows a whole lot about search engine optimization, having spent some years in that industry. Which one is it? Well, we'll give you a huge hint: His initials are S.B., he's swum a relay across the English Channel, and he's got noticeably less hair than the other guy does. Go ahead—turn to the rear cover and check out the author photos you'll find there. We'll wait right here until you get back.

Got it? Great, let's keep going. This particular individual is **passionate about laziness in his chosen field**—which means he does a good job of leveraging what he knows about a process he's already quite familiar with and likes thinking about. In his case, that happens to be selling. (By the way, it's okay if that's not your chosen field.)

When we say this guy is **passionate about laziness in his chosen field,** what we mean is this: He knows and enjoys talking to people, which is his personal form of laziness. In his mind, talking is fun, but writing proposals isn't. While talking to people is "right down the middle of his wheel house" (that's *sports talk* meaning that talking to people in real time is a core strength and thus part of his mission), writing proposals is not. In fact, writing proposals is, in his view, a pretty frustrating exercise. His thinking is that if you write the right thing, the prospect buys—but if you write the wrong thing, the prospect doesn't buy. So, when "forced" (that is "asked") to write a proposal, he leverages his laziness... and talks the prospect into writing the proposal with him! Writing the proposal with the prospect eliminates the boring job he sucks at (creating a sparkling, impressive document on the computer) and replaces it with his passion: talking to people about why and how he can add value!

It's worth mentioning that this particular guy never would have come up with this solution had he not listened to his inner "lazy-muse," which kept whispering these seductive words in his ear: "Stay true to your laziness; find another way."

Guess what he did? He listened to that voice. Instead of returning to the prospect's office with a proposal, he returned with a proposal "worksheet" that he could use to discuss his *ideas* for the proposal. He told the prospect what he had learned about the company already, and what he assumed they were trying to accomplish by buying his service.

This kind of thing happened over and over again. Invariably, the prospects contribute their own ideas, and their own wording, about what the service should include, about their budget for that service, and about other particulars they want to see in the proposal. In other words, not unlike Tom Sawyer, this shrewd guy—you know, the one with less hair and more experience in swimming the English channel than most—has actually gotten the prospect to write the proposal! Naturally, with all that help from the prospect, the proposal is now correctly written, from the prospect's point of view—all without our hero having to go through the hated "guessing what to write" part. By extending his love of talking into the negotiating process, he has found a way to make the creation of the proposal a win-win situation for him and his customer. Both sides learn what works and what doesn't. As a result, this handsome, hair-challenged, intrepid navigator of the English channel never has to waste time doing the thing he hates and sucks at doing: writing proposals.

Once you know how to leverage what you know and do well... you can compress your process... operate at peak efficiency ... and get paid more! **But... you cannot leverage what you know and do well unless you are willing to stop and think about it on a regular basis.**

"No problem can withstand the assault of sustained thinking."

~VOLTAIRE

"Never be afraid to sit awhile and think."

**~LORRAINE HANSBERRY,
A RAISIN IN THE SUN**

*"You and I are not what we eat;
we are what we think."*

~WALTER ANDERSON

*"Invest a few moments in thinking.
It will pay good interest."*

~ AUTHOR UNKNOWN

"Thinking is like loving and dying. Each of us must do it for himself."

~ JOSIAH ROYCE

"Few people think more than two or three times a year; I have made an international reputation for myself by thinking once a week."

~ GEORGE BERNARD SHAW

Don't wimp out now—take some time to think about a process that allows you to

a) enjoy yourself

and

b) create value by identifying what should happen next.

How can you leverage your knowledge about that process? How can you use that knowledge to help others... and increase your own personal efficiency? How can you turn your particular brand of laziness into money?

_____

_____

_____

_____

_____

Leverage Your Laziness!

Principle #8:
Turning Laziness into a Successful Business

"Controlled chaos is one way to get creativity. The intensity of it, the physical rush, the intimacy creates the kind of dialogue that leads to synergy."

~ RICHARD HOLBROOKE

Do you remember the premise of the classic play and television show *The Odd Couple*? Two recently divorced men try to live together in one New York City apartment... without murdering each other. Felix—the neatnik—is a "detail" guy who lives to restore order to chaos, and finds a whole lot of chaos to work with in his roommate's unkempt apartment. Oscar—the slob—is a "big idea" guy who likes connecting to people, and can't be bothered to do the dishes or pick up the dirty clothes that he occasionally leaves lying around the living room.

Ready for a surprise? If you leave out the part where they argue about domestic issues, get on each other's nerves, aggravate each other, and almost commit homicide over whether it's spaghetti or linguine that Oscar just flung against the living room wall... Felix and Oscar represent a pretty good model for the partnership relationship you want to build into your world.

Felix and Oscar may have had mismatched personalities for living together, but Oscar *really did* need a "detail person" in his life, and Felix *really did* need a "big idea" person in his. Their big mistake, we think, was trying to live together. What they really should have done was start a company together! We're like that, too. Steve is a creative, big idea guy; Jeff is a born nurturer and implementer. Neither characteristic is necessarily better than the other, but together, we think we make for a great team—a team that comes up with terrific ideas *and* gets things done.

All of us, whether we realize it or not, have limitations and blind spots that a good business partner can fill. For us, the act of trying personally to compensate for those blind spots is likely to feel a whole lot like (gasp!) work. But for our partner—who knows? It could be something that he or she was born to do—like making the perfect linguine, or writing a great sports column on a deadline.

If you can find a Felix, or an Oscar, who doesn't drive you crazy, but instead compensates for your weak spots and lets you spend more time doing what you know you do well ... think about establishing a partnership relationship with that person. This shouldn't be your "twin"—it should be someone who actually complements your unique array of strengths, weaknesses, and interests. You're looking for the accountant to match up with your "born salesperson," the driving, goal-oriented visionary to match up with your born administrator, the music to match up with your words.

Interestingly, many of the entrepreneurs and executives we've talked with over the years have considered the task of finding the right partner as being similar to the process of finding the right spouse. In fact, many people we've talked with have told us that the process of locating the right partner is *more important* than the process of finding the right spouse! Why? Because you are likely to spend more time at work on any given day than at home.

That's a debatable point, perhaps, but this one isn't: *If you're going to be lazy, you need a LAZINESS PARTNER, someone who covers for you on the stuff you suck at and helps you see and do things that you don't usually see and do optimally on your own.*

Great work often gets done in pairs. Have you noticed? That's because the partners cover each other's weaknesses and blind spots—and let each other focus on the items that belong in their own private "zone."

Who will be Lennon to your McCartney? Jobs to your Wozniak? Felix to your Oscar? You don't have to move in with the person, of course. You definitely *don't* have to let him, or her, take over your apartment... and if you ever spot your partner flinging hot pasta around the house during a disagreement, it's probably time to rethink your choice.

Once you have someone in mind, ask yourself: Does this person have the greatest potential for powerful *synergy* with me?

"A synergy describes the situation where different entities cooperate advantageously for a final outcome. If used in a business application, the word means that teamwork will produce an overall better result than if each person was working toward the same goal individually.... (Specifically, synergy is:)

- A dynamic state in which combined action is favored over the difference of individual component actions.
- Behavior of whole systems unpredicted by the behavior of their parts taken separately
- The cooperative action of two or more stimuli, resulting in a different or greater response than that of the individual stimuli."
  —Wikipedia

Leverage Your Laziness!

Principle #9:
Outsource It!

"He who rejects change is the architect of decay. The only human institution which rejects progress is the cemetery."

~ Harold Wilson

J ane was an accomplished attorney who ran her own private practice, and had reached a turning point in her career. She knew she was really good at what she did for her clients... and she also knew she had hit an income plateau. She felt she should be earning more than she was.

She went to an executive coach. "What's wrong with me?" she asked the coach. "Why can't I grow my business beyond this stage? Why am I having challenges hitting my financial goals?"

The coach said, "Do you really want to know the answer to those questions?"

Jane said, "Absolutely."

"Okay," the coach said. "Take this sheet of paper and fill it in during the day tomorrow." He handed her a grid-like worksheet with the words TIME LOG on the top. It had a little space for every quarter-hour of the day. "Record what you do in every fifteen-minute increment for a full day," the coach said. "Then meet me back here next week. Bring the sheet, so we can discuss it."

Jane had a feeling she knew where this was going, but she also had a feeling she wasn't going to make the change she needed to make in her life without completing the exercise with her coach. So she went ahead and followed his instructions. She spent a whole day filling in the blanks, tracking her behavior from seven in the morning, when she started work, to 5:30 at night, which was when she stopped. Then she brought the completed sheet to her coach for their next meeting.

"Okay, let's take a look," said the coach. "It says here that the first thing you did was stuff and lick envelopes and send them out."

"Right," said Jane. "Those were some invoices that I was about a week behind on."

"Got it," said the coach. "How much would you pay per hour for an assistant to run an accounting program that would do to that for you, do you think?"

There was a little pause.

"Maybe eighteen bucks an hour," Jane said.

"Good to know," said the coach. "Now this other line here says that you took a client call from eight to nine a.m. How much do you get paid per hour for that call?"

"About three hundred fifty dollars an hour," said Jane.

"Which do you enjoy doing more—stuffing envelopes or talking to clients?"

"No contest," said Jane. "I hate stuffing envelopes. I love talking to clients."

"Hmm ..." said the coach. "What about this line here that says 'Making photocopies and collating reports.' You did that for half an hour. How much would it cost you per hour to get an assistant who could do that for you?"

"Again, about eighteen dollars an hour," Jane said.

"Do you particularly enjoy making photocopies and collating reports?"

"No—it's incredibly boring."

"Okay, so this next activity here," the coach said, "where you spent another two hours meeting with a client in your office—how much did you earn from those two hours?"

"Seven hundred dollars," Jane replied.

"And I'm guessing you enjoyed the meeting? Or, at any rate, found it more fulfilling than making copies?"

"Yeah, it was a very good meeting."

"Are you seeing a pattern emerge here, Jane?" the coach asked.

"I think I am," said Jane.

"The real question," the coach said, leaning forward in his chair, "is how many three-hundred-and fifty-dollar hours are you going to give up to perform eighteen-dollar-an-hour chores *that you don't enjoy doing?*"

What you want, of course, is for the average dollars per hour you earn during the work day to be as high a number as possible. There's only one way to make that happen—and that's to spend more time doing what you do really well, and get paid most for doing... and less time doing things you're not so good at, and could pay someone else to do for less. Who knew? The things you do really well, and get paid most for, are typically the things you enjoy the most!

The message from Jane's coach was direct: "Find someone to outsource the eighteen-dollar-an-hour stuff to. If you can do that, you'll focus your day better, spend more time doing what you know you actually enjoy doing, be more effective... and feel less stressed at the end of the day."

"I should have been able to figure this out myself," Jane said. "Hey, remind me—how much am I paying you per hour?" she asked.

"Two hundred dollars," the coach said.

She smiled. "It was worth it," she said.

Eliminate low-value activities from your day. Outsource them to other people who are better at doing things you suck at (or, even worse, don't enjoy doing). When in doubt, ask yourself: How much would someone else pay me to do this? How much would they pay me to do what I'm really good at? Eliminate the low-paying hourly jobs you don't do well—and tend to do slowly. Replace low-wage work with high-income work!

Leverage Your Laziness!

Principle #10:
Fire The People Who Make Your Life Suck

"Change always comes bearing gifts."

~ PRICE PRITCHETT

*P*icture your favorite client—the one you love spending time with and can't wait to connect with again. Now picture all your other clients—the ones you wish were that much fun to work with.

Did you feel an emotional change just now—for the worse? How often do you put yourself through that kind of change in a given week? Month? Year?

Is it really worth it?

DOES THIS RELATIONSHIP SUCK?

Is there a particular client, employee, or vendor who always seems to bring more trouble than he or she is worth? Is there someone who always makes you feel like you're working too hard, just by talking to them? Is there someone in your world you always dread calling or meeting with? Is there someone who regularly keeps you from getting "into your zone?" Is there a boss you know you're never, ever going to be able to get along with?

If your answer to any of these questions is "yes," you should consider firing that person. Someone who is a pain in your posterior is almost certainly making it harder for you to leverage your laziness... and is also making it more likely for you to get distracted by things you suck at doing. Like managing a stupid relationship that isn't working.

If you possibly can, fire the people who make your life suck.

Understand: We're not saying you should fire people with whom you have an occasional disagreement. We're saying you should fire the people who, time and time again, make your life miserable and keep you from doing what you do best.

Seriously. Why not fire them?

Why not fire the client who's consuming all your resources and not delivering the revenue to justify all that time and effort? There's another client out there waiting for you who represents more value for both sides, and whom you'll actually look forward to talking to and working with.

Why not fire the employee who's keeping you from recruiting someone who will be even more productive, and won't make your stomach churn? That toxic relationship is not only affecting you, you know—it's affecting your entire business. It's too expensive!

Why not fire the vendor who's keeping you awake at night? If the relationship is costing you your own ability to spend time "in the zone"... it's too expensive!

Why not fire the boss who doesn't treat you with respect and deserve your talents? If what is familiar is costing you your own ability to perform at peak levels—it's too expensive!

Yes, there are times when you run into someone you probably can't cut ties with, like a brother-in-law. There are times when you have occasional, passing difficulties with someone you shouldn't fire, like a great employee who has a difference of opinion about how to attain an important goal. Neither of those situations should keep you from spending most of your time with people who help you feel like you're on top of your game.

And that's what this is really all about: how you feel. When we say "fire people you don't like," what we mean is, "manage your relationships so as to align yourself, as often as possible, with the people who are most likely to put you in your zone and make you feel great."

ARE YOU IN IT FOR THE LONG HAUL?

Of course, this may take more than a day or two to pull off. That's okay. You're in this for the long haul, right? Start making incremental progress. Start with baby steps if you need to, but decide who you're going to fire first and then, do it!

Why not?

Why not commit, right now, to get as much time as possible with the people who make you feel like you're hardly working at all? Why not spend most of your day with the people who help you get the best from yourself? Why not make it your goal to invest as much of your precious time and energy as possible in the relationships that, more often than not, really make you feel like you're doing what you were born to do? You know the type of relationship we're talking about... supportive, nurturing and empowering!

Don't wimp out! Fire the people who consistently take you out of your zone. If you can't fire them all at one time, settle for firing them one at a time.

Leverage Your Laziness!

Principle #11:
Refuse To Pay The Dead Relationship Tax!

"You need to surround yourself with quality human beings who are intelligent and have a vision."

~ VINCE MCMAHON

Congratulations! You've moved on, by following the advice in Principle #10. You've identified a relationship that wasn't working for you, and was causing you to focus on things that distracted you, aggravated you, or simply reminded you of things that you suck at doing. You're not spending time with that person now, either on the phone, in person, or by means of any high-tech communication device. You are on the path... but beware! Believe it or not, you're the one who's most likely to re-hire that person, simply by thinking about past traumas, difficulties, personality conflicts, and other treasured memories you accumulated together. Once you fire someone who is taking you out of your zone... you have to make sure the person stays fired—inside your own head.

It is too much work to let a dead relationship live on in your head. Mentally firing someone is just as important, and probably more important, than ending the relationship itself. If you don't follow up by mentally firing that person who was hijacking your time and attention, you may end up paying the Dead Relationship Tax.

This is one tax you definitely want to evade. No one gets to drive you nuts, and that goes double for every relationship you've officially decided to put behind you. The crazy boss, the neurotic ex spouse, the client from Hell—whoever it is you've decided to fire, you're not done firing them until you've well and truly disengaged from the habit of obsessing over the relationship. If you're still stewing over the problems in that now-extinct relationship with your morning coffee, you're letting the person live in your head rent-free!

Guess what? When you replay all the problems you formerly had with the person you used to get all traumatized over... your central nervous system can't tell the difference! It thinks you've still got the daily, soul-sucking drama to address with that person... and as a result, you still do. Even if you're no longer physically taking calls from that make-you-crazy person, if your central nervous system is taking imaginary calls, the toxic relationship is alive and well. Get rid of it for good.

Hold a little ceremony that officially marks your release from the clutches of that relationship that wasn't worth your time, attention or energy. Rip up a photograph. Play a special song. Drink a mason jar filled with the person's blood under the full moon. Just kidding about that last one—but do find some way to mark the end of the relationship, both externally and internally. Until you get the person out of your head, the relationship is not yet over—and you're still paying the Dead Relationship Tax!

> **Don't wimp out! Once you fire someone, create a ritual for yourself, make the firing permanent, and move on.**

"A graduation is a small but significant tradition that everyone of every age should take part in."

~ **MARTIN STOLEMAN**

"Sometimes you have to get to know someone really, really well to realize you're strangers."

~ **MARY TYLER MOORE**

"Courage is not the absence of fear, but simply moving on with dignity despite that fear."

~**PAT RILEY**

Leverage Your Laziness!

Principle #12:
Find Ginger!

*"Remember, Ginger Rogers did everything
Fred Astaire did, but backwards, wearing
a girdle, and in high heels."*

~ BOB THAVES, "FRANK AND ERNEST", 1982

Here's the good news. You're in the zone now. You now know exactly what your strong suit is. If you were Fred Astaire, you'd know that your strong suit is dancing. In fact, if you were Astaire and someone were to ask you to take a job as an architect, or a plumber, or a piano tuner, you'd know that, regardless of what you might have ended up doing for whatever reason in the short term, between dancing engagements, what you were really all about was one thing: dancing. (We covered that much in Chapters 1 through 8, if you'll recall. If you don't recall, and don't feel like you know what your strong suit is, go back and take another look at those chapters.)

You also know, thanks to the two chapters you just completed, who you *don't* want in your act. If you happened to be Fred Astaire, working the vaudeville circuit around, say, 1915, and someone happened to walk up to you and ask you to incorporate a singing poodle into your solo dance routine, you'd not only know enough to take a pass on the tuneful pooch, (Chapter 10) but you'd also know enough not to lose any sleep, worry, time, or energy resenting the poodle for trying to horn in on your act (Chapter 11).

As we say, you're definitely in the zone if you've made it this far in the book.

But ...

...if you happened to be Fred Astaire, you'd still be missing something crucial—namely, a dancing partner. You're still in search of Ginger Rogers—the partner whose strong suit complements, but does not duplicate, yours, and who can do everything you do, only backwards, wearing a girdle, and in high heels.

Okay, we admit it. The metaphor only goes so far. You don't actually *have* to pick a partner who follows you around everywhere and wears high heels and a girdle—unless, of course, those qualities are high on your list of preferences for some deeply personal reason.

Most people reading this book are not going to be looking for a dancing partner—but a business partner or a creative partner. Selecting that partner is not a matter of whim or fancy. It's something you should do only after considered thought about who *you* are, what *your* strengths and weaknesses are, and what "blind spots" *you* think are going to be most important for you to compensate for as you move forward. Who will be Rogers to your Astaire? Katharine Hepburn once said of the famous dancing duo, "He gives her class and she gives him sex." That didn't come out quite the way Hepburn meant it to, but you get the idea.

Who will be Paul McCartney (romance, senti-mentality, tradition) to your John Lennon (sexuality, cynicism, skepticism for authority and convention)? Or Lennon to your McCartney, for that matter? Who will do the things you suck at, and hate doing? Who loves doing that stuff? Who will balance your weak spots so perfectly, and add strong points that are so complementary to yours, that the two of you can accomplish things together that would be absolutely impossible for you to accomplish separately? In a recent interview, Sir Paul said that when he and John sat down to write a song it typically took *no longer than* three hours. Think about that one: no more than three hours from start to finish... for a Beatles tune. Not bad. It's amazing what you can accomplish when you're in the zone—and working with someone who complements you!

Before you even begin to think of candidates for the job of Ginger Rogers (or Paul McCartney), answer the following questions about yourself to the best of your ability. Be honest—you're under oath.

- I love social situations and enjoy interacting with people as much as possible. (T/F)

- I have a good head for figures and like solving math problems. (T/F)
- I love troubleshooting technical issues and figuring out why something works or doesn't work. (T/F).
- I'm good with words, especially the written word. (T/F)
- I love public speaking, or any other situation that allows me to be the center of attention or draw an audience. (T/F)
- I'm a "big picture" person. I usually prefer to leave details to others. (T/F)
- Tradition and precedent are important to me. (T/F)
- I'm willing to take calculated risks. (T/F)
- I'm all about the bottom line. (T/F)
- People need to respect my aesthetic sense or artistic vision. (T/F)
- I can overcome any obstacle. (T/F)
- I'm confident in my ability to manage money responsibly. (T/F)
- I love building and supporting teams, and am good at motivating others. (T/F)

- I am more organized than most people I know. (T/F)
- My computer skills are better than most people I know (T/F)

Don't wimp out! Answer the questions above to the best of your ability, then move on to the next chapter, so you can get clearer on the kind of partner you're looking for.

"When an enterprise has equal partners, then fear not."

~ Aeschylus

Leverage Your Laziness!

Principle #13:
Reality Check!

"Drive thy business, let not that drive thee."

~ **BENJAMIN FRANKLIN**

J ust out of curiosity: Did you wimp out and skip the questions in the previous chapter without answering them? If so, that's a clear signal that you haven't yet found Ginger. You need someone in your world who's better at filling out pesky questionnaires on your behalf ... or, at the very least, someone who will start giving you grief when you try to skip over important stuff, and make sure you follow through before moving on to the next chapter.

Just in case.... Consider us Ginger.

The Traits You Have, The Traits You Don't: What Are Your Strengths?

1. Gregariousness
2. Number ability
3. Technical troubleshooting
4. Written language skills
5. Public speaking
6. Big picture/vision
7. Sensitivity to tradition/precedent/procedure
8. Willingness to take calculated risks
9. Bottom line orientation
10. Aesthetics/artistic sensibility
11. Perseverence
12. Money management ability
13. Social and teambuilding skills; ability to motivate others
14. Organizational skills
15. Computer fluency

Ginger says:

1. If you DON'T love social situations and enjoy interacting with people ... you probably would benefit from a business relationship with someone who loves connecting with others.

2. If you DON'T have a good head for figures and/or like solving math problems... you probably would benefit from an alliance with someone who can, you know, figure out a restaurant tip and balance a checkbook.

3. If you DON'T love troubleshooting technical issues and figuring out why something works or doesn't work ... you definitely need someone in your life with this skill. Who knows? The fuse may blow or something.

4. If you AREN'T good with words, especially the written word ... back away from the word processor.

5. If you DON'T love public speaking or other opportunities to "STEAL THE

SPOTLIGHT" ...you need someone in your world who lives to step in front of the audience, center stage.

6. If you're NOT a "big picture" person, the kind of person who usually prefers to leave details to others... you may think you don't need such a person in your world. You're wrong. The "big picture" person can summarize your whole world into one killer sentence. This is definitely something you're going to want to connect with someone about. You know those boring meetings where people ramble on and on and on, and won't shut up, and simply refuse to get to the point, until you find yourself checking your watch for the fifth time in ten minutes, and you start having fantasies about what you could possibly do to escape—like chew your own arm off? You don't want to be the person who inspires those fantasies. Find a "big picture" person who can deliver your message.

7. If tradition, procedure, and precedent AREN'T important to you ... good luck dealing with the IRS. You may need to get someone on your side who can handle this stuff.

8. If you're NOT willing to take calculated risks... you need to talk to someone once in a while who can help you expand your risk profile intelligently.

9. If you're NOT all about the bottom line... you're definitely going to want some kind of relationship with a person who is.

10. If you DON'T CARE whether the aesthetics work... then your web site and promotional materials probably suck, and you need to talk to someone about that.

11. If you DON'T FEEL that you can overcome any obstacle ... you need someone on your side who does feel that way. Then, when the appropriate time comes, you can explain to that person why leaping off the cliff without a parachute may not be the best strategic plan.

12. If you're NOT confident in your ability to manage money responsibly... get ready for someone to volunteer to manage your money IRRESPONSIBLY. Seriously—you need someone who can handle the dollars and cents.

13. If you DON'T love building and supporting teams, and are NOT good at motivating others ... you probably will find it impossible to build an organization, or even a network, without someone who is a "people person."

14. If you AREN'T well organized ... get ready to watch any good idea you have die on the vine as you grapple with a thousand other "top priorities."

15. If you DON'T have good computer skills... prepare to lose the competitive advantage to someone who does.

And now... a word from the reality-based community. **If you feel you are actually strong in any of the areas above, ask yourself, "WHAT EXPERIENCE**

OR PROOF DO I HAVE THAT I ACTUALLY PULLED THIS OFF IN THE PAST?" If you don't have any such proof... guess what? You need help from Ginger in that area. Holding yourself responsible for something you actually suck at doing is a recipe for disaster.

Before you move on to the next chapter, make sure you have identified at least THREE areas, from the fifteen you just read, where you know for sure that you need help. If you think you *don't* need help in three different areas, keep looking... and remember what they always say about denial: it ain't just the name of a river.

_____

_____

_____

_____

_____

_____

With any luck, you are now looking in at least three areas where you know you have holes to fill. In fact, if you're really lucky, you may have more than three. You may not be certain that any one person could actually fill all the holes. Don't panic! Read on.

Leverage Your Laziness!

Principle #14:
The Mutual
"We Suck"
Zone

*"The most important single central fact about
a free market is that no exchange takes place
unless both parties benefit."*

~ **MILTON FRIEDMAN**

Y ou now know what Ginger can give you. But
what if you find out Ginger doesn't give you
everything you need?

Is that a crisis? Of course not. Relax: This is not a marriage. It's more important! (Or at least likely to consume more hours in your day.)

Your connection with your business or creative partner can, and should, grow stronger once you start "seeing other people" to fill in some of the other gaps you've identified together. Just make sure you and your partner both know exactly what you are expecting from your relationship with each other, why it benefits both sides, and what the basic ground rules are going to be.

Specifically, you and your business or creative partner should both...

- Accept that your primary shared goal is not to "have to" do anything either partner feels he or she sucks at doing. This is a two-way street. You must respect your partner's assessments about this.
- Fill at least three important, high-profile "blind spots" for each other, as identified in the previous chapter.
- Enjoy each other's company enough to make work feel like play most of the time.

- Be comfortable sharing important goals with each other, and discussing your mutual commitment to turning them into realities, including a "by when" date.
- Refuse to take things too seriously.
- Agree to invest some time. (How much time is up to the two of you.)
- Agree to get out of each other's faces when necessary. (When this is necessary is up to the two of you.)
- Be completely honest with each other about how much money is being spent, when it is being spent, and why it is being spent. The bookkeeping must always be clear to both partners, and the conversations about money must always be transparent.

Once all eight of those basic principles are in place... you're rolling. Now your job becomes a long-term one: Who else can help us to fill the remaining gaps? Who else can we connect with who has skills that will compensate for the things that we know for sure we suck at doing?

Make a list of at least three things that you know for sure that you absolutely, positively, suck at doing—and that you believe your creative or business partner also sucks at doing. Share this list with your partner and make sure he or she agrees that it's on target.

Your list of items in this MUTUAL "WE SUCK" ZONE might include:

- Making sense of the scribbles and crumpled receipts you call your bookkeeping file
- Calling prospective new customers without making them feel like they're being stalked
- Summarizing new projects and updating the website, which we last did, let's see, back in the cretaceous era.

ONCE YOU BOTH AGREE ON YOUR MUTUAL "WE SUCK" ZONE... look for people who specialize in whatever needed skills are on your list, and set a target date for when you'll track those people down by. The missing skills could be resuscitating moribund accounting departments, prospecting for new business, bringing the web site up to date, or anything else you both suck at doing. You can fill the gaps the old-fashioned way by actually talking to people face-to-face at social gatherings... or you can do it the up-to-date, LAZY way by posting the skills you are looking for on interactive on-line sites like Facebook, Linkedin, or Craigslist. It's up to you!

If you think you have no gaps to fill... if you believe you and your partner cover ALL of each other's bases perfectly... if you believe that there is NOTH-ING on your MUTUAL "WE SUCK" ZONE list... then you are either Superman or, most likely, deeply delusional. On the off-chance that you aren't Super-man, (and very few of us are) make this list and start looking for new relationships that help you to address the gaps you've identified.

Leverage Your Laziness!

Principle #15: Do Not Recruit Toxic Goons

There's a particular sub-species of negative individual you have to be particularly careful to avoid when filling your "WE SUCK" zones—people who may reach out to you as allies, but who will eventually make it virtually impossible to leverage your laziness. These folks are, alas, programmed to try to make themselves, and other people, do things that they suck at doing. We call them Toxic Goons. They are, whether they realize it consciously or not, out to sabotage themselves and virtually every relationship they enter into, and they have developed a host of extremely creative ways of doing just that.

For reasons you don't even want to know about, they specialize in finding new holes in the floor that they can fall through while holding someone else's hand...YOURS! Don't be the hand they're holding when they plummet.

Theirs isn't a rational process, but rather an obsession that compels them, usually without quite realizing what they're doing, to suck the energy and good will out of relationships. It's as if toxic goons consider putting themselves, and other people, into unresourceful states of mind to be their life's work. Once you know that you're good at X, but you suck at Y... and particularly if you've spent years figuring out that you want to focus on X, and not Y... a toxic goon is eventually going to come along and find a way to build into their relationship with you some stipulation that you must spend at least half of your time doing Y, not X. These people have built some version of the same crazy, booby-trapped world for themselves: that which they hate to do, or aren't particularly good at doing, they inevitably find some way to demand of themselves.

Toxic goons move from emergency to emergency. They are drama queens who come in both genders, power-trippers who may come off as supremely vulnerable, and victims who find subtle ways to play the role of aggressor. You know who we're talking about. They're the folks who make life miserable—for a living. And they make it almost impossible for you to stay in your zone.

By the way, if you can avoid falling in love with one of these people, that's probably a good idea, too.

Toxic goons—be they clients, bosses, relatives, or significant others—are a little like zombies. They themselves have become one of the walking dead. They're trying to see how many other people they can talk into settling for zombie-hood. Decline the invitation.

It takes a little practice and discipline to learn to recognize toxic goons. They come in all genders, shapes, sizes, and income levels. But once you do recognize one of them (their trail of broken and/ or perpetually unsettled business and personal relationships is usually a pretty good clue), you must run in the other direction, no matter how tempting the deal they offer you may seem to be. The deal is never good. The deck is always stacked... against both you and the toxic goon! So do yourself a favor, get out your hammer and pound a stake directly through the goon's morale-crushing heart.

An author we know wrote a whole book on overcoming adversity... but, as he was writing it focused his own mind, perpetually, not on solutions but on crisis, trauma and betrayal. Everyone directly connected to any of his projects quickly got "indoctrinated" in the power of negative thinking... and he quickly found creative ways for each of his "allies" to let him down. The game was rigged, as the games always are when you play with toxic goons.

There are some people in life you can't *not* let down. It's as though they're constantly auditioning for the role of Partner In Dysfunction.

Don't even show up at the auditions.

Maya Angelou once wrote, "When someone shows you who they are, believe them." We think she was writing about toxic goons.

FOUR PROVEN WAYS TO AVOID TOXIC GOONS

1. Do a 360-degree evaluation on any potential new ally. Call past clients, employees, and vendors. Get the straight scoop. If anything you hear reminds you of a toxic goon with whom you've worked in the past, run.

2. Be wary of brand-new allies who are extremely charismatic at the beginning of the relationship. They may present a very different face in due time.

3. Make a list of traits that match up with past toxic goons you've encountered. Notice these traits whenever you see them in potential business allies, and remind yourself as many times as necessary that, for some odd reason, God made it easy for us to attract the same kinds of toxic goons into our lives over and over again. It often takes a great deal of conscious effort to avoid them.

4. The lesson of this chapter is not "I must do everything myself." Keep reaching out to new people. For every toxic goon you successfully avoid engagement with, someone else more inspiring and energizing is waiting to be discovered.

Leverage Your Laziness!

Principle #16: Keep The Fire Burning!

"If you see success, it will happen."

~ PAUL MAYTORENA

You've probably gathered by now that a big part of leveraging your laziness lies in leveraging your relationships. And if for some strange reason you haven't gathered that point from what we've covered thus far, we're going to take this opportunity to beat that point into you with large wooden mallets.

Here it comes: You can't expect to leverage your laziness in isolation. You will always need other people if you hope to pull this off.

Some of the people in your circle are going to make it somewhat easier to focus on the lifelong mission of doing what you do best and avoiding what you suck at doing. Some of the people you know are going to have no real impact on that mission. Some other people are going to be (let's face it) major obstacles or distractions to that mission. And a few—a tiny minority of the total number of people with whom you're likely to interact over the course of a given week—will really light your fire and help you to recommit to that mission each and every time you interact with them.

The people in that last category are the ones who will encourage you, inspire you, challenge you, and sometimes even provoke you a bit... but they'll always respect you enough to try to get you back on track. They will never knowingly ask you to do something that they know will take you off track. And they will appreciate any help you can offer when it comes to keeping them on track. These are the people who are almost as committed as you are to making sure you get the most of the "strong suit" you were born to pursue. These are people you don't just like, but like and re- spect. These are people who share your core values, and keep sharing those values with you over time. These are people who will notice when you're spend- ing your most precious resource—time—doing some- thing you suck at doing and don't like doing. These are the folks who really and truly want to help you get your fire lit... and keep it lit.

They're precious, these people. Treasure them. Support them. Spend as much time as you possibly can with them. Help them to keep their flame of laziness alive... and you'll find that they're always there with a Zippo lighter at the moment yours starts to flicker.

The "keeper of the flame" we're talking about here may be the primary business or creative partner you've chosen for yourself... or may be one of the allies you've chosen to provide one or more of the key skills that you or your partner lack... or may even be a friend, relative, or family member whom you can count on to be there for you, in a non-judgmental way, during good times and bad. Whatever role this person plays in your life, invest time and energy consistently in support of this relationship. If you do that often enough, with enough of the right people, you will hold on to what is truly of worth in this life, and you will eventually find the task of leveraging your laziness to be (dare we say it?) easy.

"Those friends thou hast, their own true laziness prov'n, Grapple them to thy soul with hoops of steel, That they may help thee prove and improve thine."

~ WILLIAM SHAKESPEARE

Okay, okay—Shakespeare didn't write that. He wrote something similar in Act One of Hamlet, and we messed with it to make it fit at the end of this chapter, and help you remember what we were talking about. Who else besides a couple of keepers of the laziness flame would have gone to that much trouble for you—and then owned up to it?

Leverage Your Laziness!

Epilogue

"If you don't like something change it; if you can't change it, change the way you think about it."

~ **MARY ENGELBREIT**

Steve's daughter Brittany once gave him some un-expected—and wise—advice: "Life's tough—get a helmet."

We wrote this book during one of the most tumultuous, depressing, and unyieldingly bleak periods of economic downturn in our nation's history. Throughout this project, as we watched a bad economy get worse with each broadcast of the evening news, we found ourselves wondering: Could we use this challenging period of our nation's history—our world's history—as a test of our own theories? Could this stuff actually get us through a period as difficult as this one? Could we follow our own advice, walk our own talk, and come out on the other side of an economic meltdown with our smile—and our own deep personal commitment to laziness—intact?

We're happy—and proud—to report that we could.

We know, just as you know, that the new economy can be a scary place. Let's face it: There are a whole lot of unknowns to deal with, and the unknown can be intimidating. But guess what? The unknown can also be a source of power.

We believe there are two sides to any unknown situation that you may face in this life: the scary side... and the inspiring side. There are two handles you can use to "catch" any situation: the handle that's scary, or the handle that's lazy. The lazy handle is always available to you, and if you learn to grasp it and follow its momentum, you will find that it's ready to show you the path that can lead you past any obstacle: the path of energy, possibility, abundance, autonomy, self-determination—and life on your own terms.

What other terms are there?

When in doubt, choose the lazy handle—the handle that lets you be yourself. You'll not only be more likely to hit your goals ... but you'll also be a lot happier.

Steve Bookbinder

Steve Bookbinder is passionate about training, professional coaching and speaking presentations. He's logged millions of miles delivering more than 2,000 workshops and speeches to thousands of sales professionals worldwide. Steve's unique and engaging style, featuring a healthy mix of humor and personal insight, draws upon his background as an actor, athlete and swimming coach. Many of his students—including professionals at the top of their game—credit Steve and his pragmatic, action-oriented training style, for helping them to change, set new goals and achieve even stronger results. Steve's diversified training experience includes fields as diverse as digital media, broadcast and print advertising, telecommunications, information, consulting, energy, hospitality, financial services, office supplies and charitable-giving.

Steve has more than a decade of experience selling online media, search engine marketing and related advertising products. For over 20 years, he managed, trained and coached media sales executives for large and start-up media companies throughout the U.S. and Canada. He is the author and co-author of more than 25 books, articles and audio training programs, including "How to Be Your Own Coach: Six Simple Questions for Achieving Your Goals!" (www.byourowncoach.com) with Jeff Goldberg.

In addition to serving as CEO and lead instructor for Digital Media Training, Steve is an instructor for Mediabistro, where he provides search engine marketing advice to advertising agencies. He has a Bachelor of Arts in Communications from the State University of New York at Albany.

CONTACT HIM AT:

www.dmtraining.net

steve@dmtraining.net

Jeff Goldberg

Jeff Goldberg considers himself the Ralph Cramden of sales. For more than three decades he's sold, trained, coached and consulted with companies of all sizes in a wide variety of industries. Like Ralph, he spent a lot of time looking for the "easy" way to make it big. He discovered that while there's no "easy" way, success doesn't have to be hard once you figure out the rules: when to follow them, when to break them, and how to exploit them to your advantage.

A natural ham, Jeff brings a background in theater and a brief foray into the world of stand-up comedy to his career as an international speaker and trainer. He considers the day he met Steve Bookbinder to be "one of the most fortuitous events of my life," and credits much of his ability and success to Steve. Their partnership, and the way they work together, was the basis of the concept for this book.

Jeff is currently a consultant, trainer and coach to some of the world's largest and best-known organizations. He is the co-author, with Steve Bookbinder, of "How to Be Your Own Coach: Six Simple Questions for Achieving Your Goals!" (www.byourowncoach.com) He lives at (and loves) the beach. He is the father of three wonderful children and an aging pug named Dora. His goal in life is to help others do whatever it is they're trying to do better.

CONTACT HIM AT:

www.jgsalespro.com

jeff@jgsalespro.com

Lazy Thoughts

_____

_____

_____

_____

_____

_____

_____

_____

_____

_____

_____

_____

_____

_____

_____

_____